crossover Top

Yarn
Red Heart/Coats & Clark *Baby TLC*, 5oz/142g; 242yd/222m (acrylic)
5 (5) balls in #5935 Clear Blue

Crochet Hooks
Size I/9 (5.5mm) crochet hook
or size to obtain gauge
Size H/8 (5mm) crochet hook

Notions
Yarn needle
US 6 (4mm) x 48" (60")/122 (152.2)cm long circular knitting needles (optional)

Two crafts unite in this crochet shell-stitch sweater edged with knitted trim. Not a knitter? No problem—you can work the trim in crochet, instead.

Sizes
XS/S (M/L)

Finished Measurements
Bust 30 (38)"/76 (96.5)cm

Gauge
3 shells = 4"/12.5cm
10 rows = 4"/10cm
Take time to check gauge.

Notes
1 The top is constructed in 2 pieces, one for the left side and one for the right side. The 2 pieces are joined when the bottom band is worked.
2 Bust and waist measurements can be customized by overlapping panels less or more. See Waistband.

Stitch Glossary
K1 knit one
P1 purl one
M1 make one knit increase (with needle tip, lift strand between last st knit and next st on left-hand needle and knit into the back of lifted strand. One stitch has been added.
Shell work (4 dc, ch 1, 4 dc) in specified st or sp.

V-st work (dc, ch 1, dc) in specified st or sp.

Pattern Stitch
Diamond stitch
Row 1 Sc in 2nd ch from hook; * sk next 3 chs, shell in next ch, sk next 3 chs, sc in next ch; repeat from * across; ch 3, turn.
Row 2 Dc in first sc; * ch 5, sk next shell, V-st in next sc; repeat from * across to last shell; ch 5, sk last shell, 2 dc in last sc; ch 3, turn.
Row 3 Work 4 dc in first dc (½ shell made), sk next dc, sc over ch and into ch-1 sp of next shell 2 rows below; * shell in ch-1 sp of next V-st, sc over ch and into ch-1 sp of next shell 2 rows below; repeat from * across to last dc and turning ch-3; sk next dc, 5 dc in 3rd ch of turning ch-3 (½ shell made); ch 3, turn.
Row 4 Sk first 5 dc; * V-st in next sc, ch 5, sk next shell; repeat from * across to last sc; V-st in last sc, ch 2, sk next 4 dc, sl st in 3rd ch of turning ch-3; ch 1, turn.
Row 5 Sc in sl st; * shell in ch-1 sp of next V-st, sc over ch and into ch-1 sp of next shell 2 rows below; repeat from * across, ending with sc over turning ch-3 and into 5th dc 2 rows below; ch 3, turn.

Top
Panels (make 2)
Note Panels for XS and S are made the same and M and L are made the same. When directions are given for both sizes, numbers for XS and S are outside of parentheses and M and L are inside parentheses.

Front body
Starting at bottom front with I hook, ch 58 (74).
Row 1 Work Row 1 of pat st—7 (9) shells.
Row 2 Work Row 2 of pat st, ending with tr in last sc (instead of 2 dc in last sc); ch 4, turn (instead of ch 3, turn).
Row 3 Dc in tr, sc over ch and into ch-1 sp of shell 2 rows below, work Row 3 of pat st from * across—6 (8) shells and one ½ shell.
Row 4 Work Row 4 of pat st, ending with V-st in last sc; sk next dc, sc in 4th ch of turning ch-4; ch 4, turn (instead of ch 1, turn).
Row 5 Work 4 dc in ch-1 sp of next V-st (½ shell made), sc over ch and into ch-1 sp of shell 2 rows below, work Row 5 of pat st from * across—6 (8) shells and one ½ shell.
Row 6 Work Row 2 of pat st, ending with V-st in last sc; ch 2, sk next 4 dc, sl st in turning ch-4 sp; ch 1, turn (instead of ch 3, turn).
Row 7 Sc in sl st; work Row 3 of pat st from * across—6 (8) shells and one ½ shell.
Row 8 Work Row 4 of pat st across to last sc; tr in last sc; ch 4, turn (instead of ch 1, turn).
Row 9 Dc in tr, sc over ch and into ch-1 sp 2 rows below, work Row 5 of pat st from * across—6 (8) shells.
Row 10 Work Row 2 of pat st, ending with V-st in last sc; sk next dc, sl st in 4th ch of turning ch-4; ch 4, turn (instead of ch-3, turn).
Row 11 Work 4 dc in ch-1 sp of next V-st (½ shell made), sc over ch and into ch-1 sp of shell 2 rows below, work Row 3 of pat st from * across—5 (7) shells and two ½ shells.
Row 12 Work Row 4 of pat st, working sl st at end in turning ch-4 sp.
Row 13 Work Row 5 of pat st—6 (8) shells.
Rows 14–25 Repeat Rows 2–13 of Front Body. At end of Rows 15, 17 and 19—5 (7) shells and one ½ shell. At end of Rows 21 and 25—5 (7) shells. At end of Row 23—4 (6) shells and two ½ shells.
Rows 26–32 Repeat Rows 2–8 of Front Body. At end of Rows 27, 29 and 31—4 (6) shells and one ½ shell.

For XS and S only
Row 33 Repeat Row 9 of Front Body—4 shells. At end of row, ch 4, turn (instead of ch 3, turn).

For M and L only
Rows 33–37 Repeat Rows 9–13 of Front Body. At end of Row 37, ch 4, turn (instead of ch 3, turn). At end of Rows 33 and 37—6 shells. At end of Row 35—5 shells and two ½ shells.

Front armhole shaping
For XS and S only
Row 1 Work Row 2 of pat st, ending with V-st in last sc; sk next dc, sc in 4th ch of turning ch-4; ch 4, turn (instead of ch 3, turn).
Row 2 Work 4 dc in ch-1 sp of next V-st (½ shell made), sc over ch and into ch-1 sp of next shell 2 Rows below, work Row 3 of pat st from * across, ending with shell in turning ch-4 sp—4 shells and one ½ shell. Ch 4, turn (instead of ch 3, turn).
Row 3 Dc in first dc, ch 5, sk next shell, work Row 4 of pat st from * across, ending with V-st in last sc; ch 2, sk next 4 dc, sl st in turning ch-4 sp; ch 1, turn.
Row 4 Work Row 5 of pat st, ending with shell in turning ch-4 sp—5 shells.
Row 5 Dc in first dc, work Row 2 of pat st from * across, ending with tr in last sc (instead of 2 dc in last sc); ch 4, turn (instead of ch 3, turn).

For M and L only
Row 1 Work Row 2 of pat st, ending with tr in last sc; ch 4, turn (instead of ch 3, turn).
Row 2 Dc in tr, sc over ch and into ch-1 sp of shell 2 Rows below, work Row 3 of pat st from * across, ending with shell in turning ch-4 sp—6 shells. Ch 4, turn (instead of ch 3, turn).
Row 3 Dc in first dc, ch 5, sk next shell, work Row 4 of pat st from * across, ending with V-st in last sc, sk next dc, sc in 4th ch of turning ch-4; ch 4, turn (instead of ch 1, turn).
Row 4 Work 4 dc in ch-1 sp of next V-st (½ shell made), sc over ch and into ch-1 sp of next shell 2 Rows below, work Row 5 of pat st from * across, ending with shell in turning ch-4 sp—6 shells and one ½ shell.
Row 5 Dc in first dc, work Row 2 of pat st from * across, ending with V-st in last sc; ch 2, sk next 4 dc, sl st in turning ch-4 sp; ch 1, turn (instead of ch 3, turn).

Front neck shaping
For XS and S only

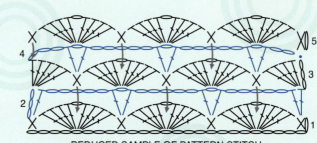
REDUCED SAMPLE OF PATTERN STITCH
DIAMOND STITCH

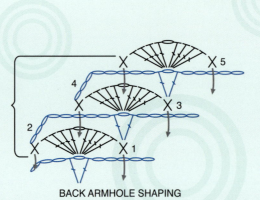
BACK ARMHOLE SHAPING

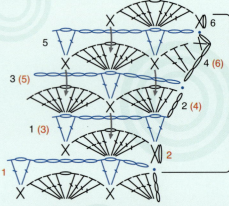
INCREASE PATTERN (BACK NECK SHAPING)
XS/S: Black row numbers
M/L: Red row numbers

BACK SHAPING PATTERNS

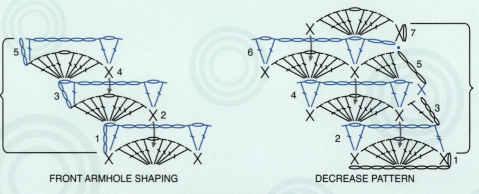
FRONT ARMHOLE SHAPING   DECREASE PATTERN
FRONT SHAPING PATTERNS

crossover Top

Rows 1–8 Repeat Rows 3–10 of Front Body. At end of Rows 1, 3 and 5—4 shells and one ½ shell. At end of Row 7—4 shells.

For M and L only
Rows 1–7 Repeat Rows 7–13 of Front Body. At end of Row 1—6 shells and one ½ shell. At end of Rows 3 and 7—6 shells. At end of Row 5—5 shells and two ½ shells.
Rows 8–12 Repeat Rows 2–6 of Front Body. At end of Rows 9 and 11—5 shells and one ½ shell.

Shoulder
For XS and S only
Row 1 Work 4 dc in ch-1 sp of next V-st (½ shell made), sc over ch and into ch-1 sp of next shell 2 rows below, work Row 3 of pat st from * across—3 shells and two ½ shells.
Row 2 Work Row 4 of pat st, ending with sl st in turning ch-4 sp.
Row 3 Work Row 5 of pat st—4 shells.
Rows 4 and **5** Work Rows 2 and 3 of pat st. At end of Row 5, 3 shells and two ½ shells.
Rows 6–19 Repeat Rows 2–5 of shoulder 3 times more, then repeat Rows 2 and 3 of shoulder once more.

For M and L only
Row 1 Sc in sl st, work Row 3 of pat st from * across—5 shells and one ½ shell.
Row 2 Work Row 4 of pat st, ending with 2 dc in last sc (instead of V-st in last sc); ch 3, turn (instead of ch 1, turn).
Row 3 Work 4 dc in first dc (½ shell made), sc over ch and into ch-1 sp of next shell 2 rows below; work Row 5 of pat st from * across—5 shells and one ½ shell .
Row 4 Work Row 2 of pat st, ending with V-st in last sc; ch 2, sk next 4 dc, sl st in 3rd ch of turning ch-3; ch 1, turn (instead of ch 3, turn).
Rows 5–19 Repeat Rows 1–4 of shoulder 3 times more, then repeat Rows 1–3 of shoulder once more.

Back neck shaping
For XS and S only
Row 1 Work Row 2 of pat st, ending with V-st in last sc.
Row 2 Work (2 dc, ch 1, 4 dc) in ch-1 sp of first V-st (¾ shell made), sc over ch and into ch-1 sp of next shell 2 rows below, work Row 3 of pat st from * across—3 shells, one ½ shell and one ¾ shell.
Row 3 Work Row 4 of pat st, ending with V-st in last sc; ch 4, sk next ¾ shell, sl st in 3rd ch of turning ch-3; ch 4, turn (instead of ch 1, turn).
Row 4 Sc in 2nd ch from hook, hdc in next ch, 2 dc in last ch (¼ shell made), sc over ch and into ch-1 sp of next ¾ shell 2 rows below, work Row 5 of pat st from * across—4 shells and one ¼ shell.
Row 5 Work Row 2 of pat st, ending with V-st in last sc; ch 2, sk next ¼ shell, sl st in skipped ch of turning ch-4; ch 1, turn (instead of ch 3, turn).
Row 6 Sc in sl st, work Row 3 of pat st from * across—4 shells and one ½ shell .
Row 7 Work Row 4 of pat st, ending with V-st in last sc; ch 3, turn (instead of ch 1, turn).
Row 8 Work (2 dc, ch 1, 4 dc) in ch-1 sp of first V-st (¾ shell made), sc over ch and into ch-1 sp of next shell 2 rows below, work Row 5 of pat st from * across—4 shells and one ¾ shell.
Row 9 Work Row 2 of pat st, ending with V-st in last sc; ch 4, sk next ¾ shell, sl st in 3rd ch of turning ch-3; ch 4, turn (instead of ch 3, turn).
Row 10 Sc in 2nd ch from hook, hdc in next ch, 2 dc in last ch (¼ shell made), sc over ch and into ch-1 sp of next ¾ shell 2 rows below, work Row 3 of pat st from * across—4 shells, one ½ shell and one ¼ shell.
Row 11 Work Row 4 of pat st, ending with V-st in last sc; ch 2, sk next ¼ shell, sl st in skipped ch of turning ch-4; ch 1, turn.

For M and L only
Rows 1 and 2 Repeat Rows 4 and 1 of shoulder. At end of Row 2—5 shells and one ½ shell .
Rows 3–7 Repeat Rows 7–11 of back neck shaping on XS and S. At end of Row 4—5 shells and one ¾ shell. At

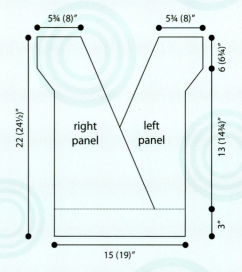

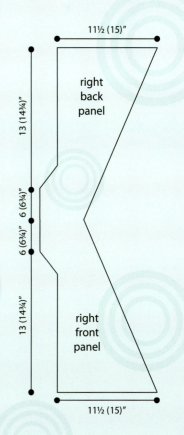

end of Row 6—5 shells, one ½ shell and one ¼ shell.
Row 8 Repeat Row 3 of shoulder on XS and S—6 shells.
Rows 9–15 Repeat Rows 1–7 of back neck shaping on XS and S. At end of Row 10—5 shells, one ¾ shell and one ½ shell. At end of Row 12—6 shells and one ¼ shell. At end of Row 14—6 shells and one ½ shell.

Back armhole shaping
For sizes XS and S only
Row 1 Work Row 5 of pat st—5 shells; ch 8, turn (instead of ch 3, turn).
Row 2 Sk first shell, V-st in next sc; work Row 2 of pat st from * across, ending with V-st in last sc.
Row 3 Work (2 dc, ch 1, 4 dc) in ch-1 sp of first V-st (¾ shell made), sc over ch and into ch-1 sp of next shell 2 rows below, work Row 3 of pat st from * across, ending with sc over ch-8 and into ch-1 sp of last shell 2 rows below—4 shells and one ¾ shell; ch 8, turn (instead of ch 3, turn).
Row 4 Work Row 4 of pat st from * across, ending with V-st in last sc; ch 4, sk next ¾ shell, sl st in 3rd ch of turning ch-3; ch 4, turn (instead of ch 1, turn).
Row 5 Sc in 2nd ch from hook, hdc in next ch, 2 dc in last ch (¼ shell made), sc over ch and into ch-1 sp of next ¾ shell 2 rows below, work Row 5 of pat st from * across, ending with sc over ch-8 and into ch-1 sp of last shell 2 rows below—4 shells and one ¼ shell.

For M and L only
Row 1 Work (2 dc, ch 1, 4 dc) in ch-1 sp of first V-st (¾ shell made), sc over ch and into ch-1 sp of next shell 2 rows below, work Row 5 of pat st from * across—6 shells and one ¾ shell; ch 8, turn (instead of ch 3, turn).
Row 2 Sk first shell, V-st in next sc; work Row 2 of pat st from * across, ending with V-st in last sc; ch 4, sk next ¾ shell, sl st in 3rd ch of turning ch-3; ch 4, turn (instead of ch 3, turn).
Row 3 Sc in 2nd ch from hook, hdc in next ch, 2 dc in last ch (¼ shell made), sc over ch and into ch-1 sp of next ¾ shell 2 rows below, work Row 3 of pat st from * across, ending with sc over ch-8 and into ch-1 sp of last shell 2 rows below—6 shells and one ¼ shell; ch 8, turn (instead of ch 3, turn).
Row 4 Sk first shell, work Row 4 of pat st from * across, ending with V-st in last sc; ch 2, sk next ¼ shell, sl st in skipped ch of turning ch-4; ch 1, turn.
Row 5 Sc in sl st, work Row 5 of pat st from * across, ending with sc over ch-8 and into ch-1 sp of last shell 2 rows below—6 shells.

Back Body
For XS and S only
Rows 1–7 Repeat Rows 5–11 of back neck shaping. At end of Row 2—4 shells and one ½ shell. At end of Row 4—4 shells and one ¾ shell. At end of Row 6—4 shells, one ½ shell and one ¼ shell.
Row 8 Work Row 5 of pat st—5 shells.
Rows 9–19 Repeat Rows 1–11 of back neck shaping. At end of Row 10—4 shells, one ¾ shell and one ½ shell. At end of Row 12—5 shells and one ½ shell. At end of Row 14—5 shells and one 1/2 shell. At end of Row 16—5 shells and one ¾ shell. At end of Row 18— 5 shells, one ½ shell and one ¼ shell.
Row 20 Work Row 5 of pat st—6 shells.

crossover Top

Rows 21–31 Repeat Rows 1–11 of back neck shaping. At end of Row 22—5 shells, one ¾ shell and one ½ shell. At end of Row 24—6 shells and one ¼ shell. At end of Row 26—6 shells and one ½ shell. At end of Row 28—6 shells and one ¾ shell. At end of Row 30—6 shells, one ½ shell and one ¼ shell.
Row 32 Work Row 5 of pat st—7 shells.

For M and L only
Rows 1–7 Repeat Rows 9–15 of back neck shaping. At end of Row 2—5 shells, one ¾ shell and one ½ shell. At end of Row 4—6 shells and one ¼ shell. At end of Row 6—6 shells and one ½ shell.
Rows 8–19 Repeat Rows 4–15 of back neck shaping. At end of Row 8—6 shells and one ¾ shell. At end of Row 10—6 shells, one ½ shell and one ¼ shell. At end of Row 12—7 shells. At end of Row 14—6 shells, one ¾ shell and one ½ shell. At end of Row 16—7 shells and one ¼ shell. At end of Row 18—7 shells and one ½ shell.
Rows 20–31 Repeat Rows 4–15 of back neck shaping. At end of Row 20—7 shells and one ¾ shell. At end of Row 22—7 shells, one ½ shell and one ¼ shell. At end of Row 24—8 shells. At end of Row 26—8 shells, one ¾ shell and one ½ shell. At end of Row 28—8 shells and one ¼ shell. At end of Row 30—8 shells and one ½ shell.
Rows 32–36 Repeat Rows 4–8 of back neck shaping. At end of Row 32—8 shells and one ¾ shell. At end of Row 34—8 shells, one ½ shell and one ¼ shell. At end of Row 36—9 shells.

For all sizes
Row 33 (37) Dc in first sc; *ch 2, sl st in ch-1 sp of next shell, ch 2, V-st in next sc; repeat from * across. Fasten off.

Finishing
Block panels to schematic sizes.

Joining
Row 1 On right panel is right side and Row 1 on left panel is wrong side to create mirror images. Fold panels in half with right sides together and first and last rows meeting. Pin side seams. Whipstitch side seams together from bottom of panel to top of armhole shaping.

Armhole edging
With right side facing, join yarn with sc to armhole opening at side seam. Work sc evenly spaced along edge of armhole. Fasten off. Repeat edging on other armhole.

Panel edging
Note Edging may be knit or crochet. Follow instructions below for the method you choose. (Knitted edging is shown in main photo; crochet edging is shown at left.)

Option #1: Crochet edging
Row 1 With right side facing and I hook, join yarn with sc at bottom of side edge of either panel, sc evenly spaced along side edge. Fasten off.
Row 2 (right side) Change to H hook. Join yarn with sc in BL of first sc on Row 1, sc in BL of same sc, sc in BL of next sc and in BL of each sc across to last sc, 2 sc in BL of last sc; ch 1, turn.
Row 3 Sc in FL of first sc and in FL of each sc across; ch 1, turn.
Row 4 2 sc in BL of first sc, sc in BL of each sc across to last sc, 2 sc in BL of last sc. Fasten off.

Option #2: Knit edging
Row 1 Work same as Row 1 on crochet waistband, but do not fasten off.
Row 2 Cast on 239 (275) sts by picking up lps along sc edge with circular knitting needles.
Rows 3 and 5 P3, K1 across, turn.
Rows 4 and 6 K1, M1, K2, P1 {K3, P1} across to last 3 sts, K2, M1, K1, turn. Bind off in pattern.

Waistband
Note Waistband can be knit or crochet. Follow directions below for the method you choose.
Lay out panels to schematic layout, overlapping panels to create a false wrap to dimensions on schematic or to your desired measurements. Pin bottom edge of panels together at overlap.

Option #1: crochet waistband
Rnd 1 With right side facing, join yarn with sc in bottom of either side seam, work 203 (251) more sc (or amount of sc for desired waitband fit) evenly spaced along bottom edge, working through both panels where they overlap—204 (252) sc; join with sl st in first sc.
Rnd 2 Change to H hook. Ch 1, sc in BL of each sc around; join with sl st in first sc. Do not turn. Repeat Rnd 2 until waistband measures 3"/7.5cm. Fasten off.

Option #2: knit waistband
Rnd 1 Work same as Row 1 on crochet waistband.
Rnd 2 With wrong side facing, picking up lps along sc edge with circular knitting needle, pick up 204 (252) sts or amount of sts for desired waistband fit making sure to have a multiple of 4 sts.
Rnd 3 K3, P1 around.
Repeat Rnd 3 until waistband measures 3"/7.5cm. Bind off in pattern.

Weave in all ends. Steam top to soften yarn and improve drape.

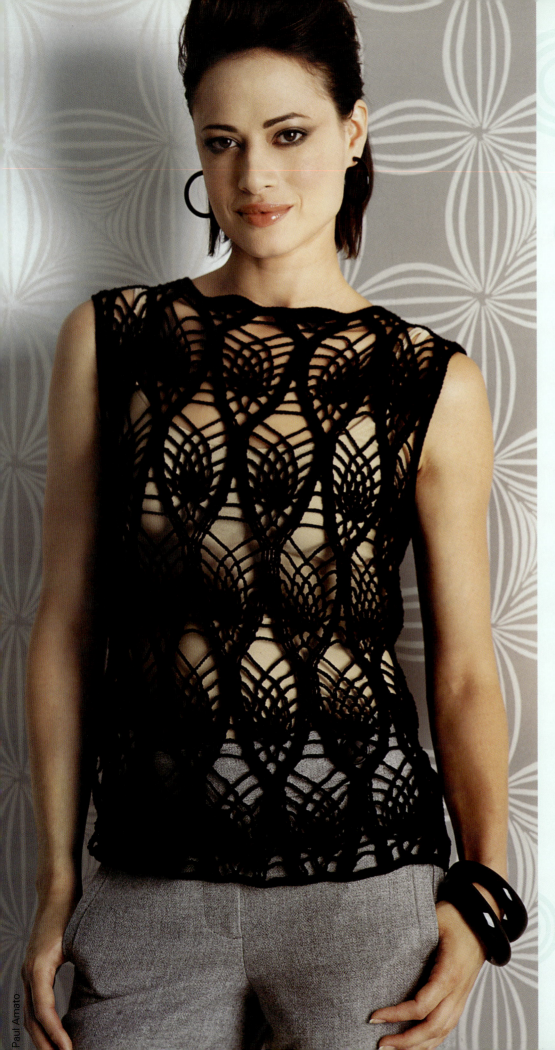

A flattering fit, versatile shape and gorgeous stitch pattern make this piece an instant classic. So go ahead, embrace the lace and stitch up this stunner!

Sizes
S/M (L/1X, 2X/3X)

Finished Measurements
Chest 42 (49, 56)"/106.5 (124.5, 142)cm
Length 23 (23½, 24)"/ 58.5 (59.5, 61)cm

Gauge
One pattern repeat (at widest point) = 3½"/9cm; 16 rows = 8½"/21.5cm over Pattern Stitch using size D/3 (3.25mm) crochet hook.
Take time to check gauge.

Stitch Glossary
tr2tog (tr 2 sts together) *Yarn over twice, insert hook in next st, yarn over and draw up a loop, [yarn over and draw through 2 loops on hook] twice; repeat from * once more, yarn over and draw through all 3 loops on hook.

Pattern Stitch
Row 1 Tr in 7th ch from hook (beginning ch counts as dtr, ch 1), ch 3, sk next 3 ch, tr in next 3 ch, ch 7, sk next 7 ch, tr in next 3 ch, ch 3, sk next 3 ch, *[tr, ch 3, tr] in next ch, ch 3, sk next 3 ch, tr in next 3 ch, ch 7, sk next 7 ch, tr in next 3 ch, ch 3, sk next 3 ch; repeat from * across to last ch, [tr, ch 1, dtr] in last ch.
Row 2 Ch 5 (counts as tr, ch 1 here and throughout), turn, tr in first ch-1 sp, [ch 1, tr in same ch-1 sp] twice, ch 1, sk next tr,

lacy Pineapples

Yarn
AUNT LYDIA'S *Fashion Crochet Thread*, Size 3, each ball approx 150yd/137m (cotton)
4 (5, 6) balls #12 Black

Crochet Hooks
Size D/3 (3.25mm) crochet hook
or size to obtain gauge

Notions
Stitch markers
Yarn needle

sk next ch-3 sp, tr in next 3 tr, ch 5, sk next ch-7 sp, tr in next 3 tr, ch 1, sk next ch-3 sp, sk next tr, *tr in next ch-3 sp, [ch 1, tr in same ch-3 sp] 6 times, ch 1, sk next tr, sk next ch-3 sp, tr in next 3 tr, ch 5, sk next ch-7 sp, tr in next 3 tr, ch 1, sk next ch-3 sp, sk next tr; repeat from * across to last ch-1 sp (formed by turning ch), tr in last ch-1 sp, [ch 1, tr in same ch-1 sp] 3 times.

Row 3 Ch 7 (counts as tr, ch 3 here and throughout), turn, sc in first ch-1 sp, [ch 6, sk next tr, sc in next ch-1 sp] twice, ch 4, sk next tr, sk next ch-1 sp, tr in next 3 tr, ch 3, sk next ch-5 sp, tr in next 3 tr, ch 4, sk next ch-1 sp, sk next tr, sc in next ch-1 sp, *[ch 6, sk next tr, sc in next ch-1 sp] 5 times, ch 4, sk next tr, sk next ch-1 sp, tr in next 3 tr, ch 3, sk next ch-5 sp, tr in next 3 tr, ch 4, sk next ch-1 sp, sk next tr, sc in next ch-1sp; repeat from * across to last 2 ch-1 sp, [ch 6, sk next tr, sc in next ch-1 sp] 2 times, ch 3, tr in last tr (formed by turning ch).

Row 4 Ch 1, turn, sc in first tr, sk first ch-3 sp, [ch 6, sk next sc, sc in next ch-6 sp] twice, ch 4, sk next sc, sk next ch-4 sp, tr in next 3 tr, ch 1, sk next ch-3 sp, tr in next 3 tr, ch 4, sk next ch-4 sp, sk next sc, sc in next ch-6 sp, *[ch 6, sk next sc, sc in next ch-6 sp] 4 times, ch 4, sk next sc, sk next ch-4 sp, tr in next 3 tr, ch 1, sk next ch-3 sp, tr in next 3 tr, ch 4, sk next ch-4 sp, sk next sc, sc in next ch-6 sp; repeat from * across to last 2 ch-sp, ch 6, sk next sc, sc in next ch-6 sp, ch 6, sc in last tr (formed by turning ch).

Row 5 Ch 7, turn, sc in first ch-6 sp, ch 6, sk next sc, sc in next ch-6 sp, ch 5, sk next sc, sk next ch-4 sp, tr in next 2 tr, tr2tog (sk ch-1 sp between the next 2 tr when working the tr2tog), tr in next 2 tr, ch 5, sk next ch-4 sp, sk next sc, sc in next ch-6 sp, *[ch 6, sk next sc, sc in next ch-6 sp] 3 times, ch 5, sk next sc, sk next ch-4 sp, tr in next 2 tr, tr2tog (sk ch-1 sp between the next 2 tr when working the tr2tog), tr in next 2 tr, ch 5, sk next ch-4 sp, sk next sc, sc in next ch-6 sp; repeat from * to last ch-6 sp, ch 6, sk next sc, sc in last ch-6 sp, ch 3, tr in last sc.

Row 6 Ch 1, turn, sc in first tr, ch 6, sk first ch-3 sp, sk next sc, sc in next ch-6 sp, ch 6, sk next sc, sk next ch-5 sp, tr in next 5 tr, ch 6, sk next ch-5 sp, sk next sc, sc in next ch-6 sp, *[ch 6, sk next sc, sc in next ch-6 sp] twice, ch 6, sk next sc, sk next ch-5 sp, tr in next 5 tr, ch 6 sk next ch-5 sp, sk next sc, sc in next ch-6 sp; repeat from * across to last ch-sp, ch 6, sc in last tr (formed by turning ch).

Row 7 Ch 7, turn, sc in first ch-6 sp, ch 7, sk next sc, sk next ch-6 sp, tr in next 5 tr, ch 7, sk next ch-6 sp, sk next sc, sc in next ch-6 sp, *ch 6, sk next sc, sc in next ch-6 sp, ch 7, sk next sc, sk next ch-6 sp, tr in next 5 tr, ch 7, sk next ch-6 sp, sk next sc, sc in next ch-6 sp; repeat from * across to last sc, ch 3, tr in last sc.

Row 8 Ch 1, turn, sc in first tr, ch 8, sk first ch-3 sp, sk next sc, sk next ch-7 sp, tr in next 2 tr, [tr, ch 5, tr] in next tr, tr in next 2 tr, ch 8, sk next ch-7 sp, sk next sc, *sc in next ch-6 sp, ch 8, sk next sc, sk next ch-7 sp, tr in next 2 tr, [tr, ch 5, tr] in next tr, tr in next 2 tr, ch 8, sk next ch-7 sp, sk next sc; repeat from * to last tr, sc in last tr (formed by turning ch).

Row 9 Ch 11, turn, sk first sc, sk next ch-8 sp, tr in next 3 tr, ch 3, [tr, ch 3, tr] in next ch-5 sp, ch 3, tr in next 3 tr, *ch 7, sk next 2 ch-8 sps, tr in next 3 tr, ch 3, [tr, ch 3, tr] in next ch-5 sp, ch 3, tr in next 3 tr; repeat from * to last ch-8 sp, ch 3, yarn over 6 times, insert hook in last sc, yarn over and draw up a loop, [yarn over and draw through 2 loops on hook] 7 times.

Row 10 Ch 6, turn, sk first ch-3 sp, tr in next 3 tr, ch 1, sk next ch-3 sp, sk next tr, tr in next ch-3 sp, [ch 1, tr in same ch-3 sp] 6 times, ch 1, sk next tr, sk next ch-3 sp, tr in next 3 tr, *ch 5, sk next ch-7 sp, tr in next 3 tr, ch 1, sk next ch-3 sp, sk next tr, tr in next ch-3 sp, [ch 1, tr in same ch-3 sp] 6 times, ch 1, sk next tr, sk next ch-3 sp, tr in next 3 tr; repeat from * across to turning ch, ch 2, sk 3 ch of turning ch, tr in next ch.

Row 11 Ch 5, turn, sk first ch-2 sp, tr in next 3 tr, ch 4, sk next ch-1 sp, sk next tr, sc in next ch-1 sp, [ch 6, sk next tr, sc in next ch-1 sp] 5 times, ch 4, sk next tr, sk next ch-1 sp, tr in next 3 tr, *ch 3, sk next ch-5 sp, tr in next 3 tr, ch 4, sk next ch-1 sp, sk next tr, sc in next ch-1sp, [ch 6, sk next tr, sc in next ch-1 sp] 5 times, ch 4, sk next tr, sk next ch-1 sp, tr in next 3 tr; repeat from * across to last ch-2 sp, ch 1, sk last ch-2 sp, tr in last tr (formed by turning ch).

Row 12 Ch 4 (counts as tr here and throughout), sk first ch-1 sp, tr in next 3 tr, ch 4, sk next ch-4 sp, sk next sc,

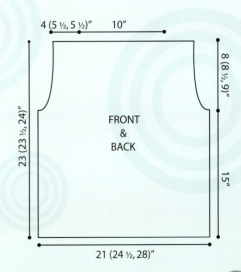

4 (5 ½, 5 ½)"   10"

FRONT & BACK

23 (23 ½, 24)"

8 (8 ½, 9)"

15"

21 (24 ½, 28)"

9

sc in next ch-6 sp, [ch 6, sk next sc, sc in next ch-6 sp] 4 times, ch 4, sk next sc, sk next ch-4 sp, tr in next 3 tr, *ch 1, sk next ch-3 sp, tr in next 3 tr, ch 4, sk next ch-4 sp, sk next sc, sc in next ch-6 sp, [ch 6, sk next sc, sc in next ch-6 sp] 4 times, ch 4, sk next sc, sk next ch-4 sp, tr in next 3 tr; repeat from * across to last ch-1 sp, sk last ch-1 sp, tr in last tr (formed by turning ch).
Row 13 Ch 4, turn, sk next tr, tr in next 2 tr, ch 5, sk next ch-4 sp, sk next sc, sc in next ch-6 sp, [ch 6, sk next sc, sc in next ch-6 sp] 3 times, ch 5, sk next sc, sk next ch-4 sp, tr in next 2 tr, *tr2tog (sk ch-1 sp between the next 2 tr when working the tr2tog), tr in next 2 tr, ch 5, sk next ch-4 sp, sk next sc, sc in next ch-6 sp, [ch 6, sk next sc, sc in next ch-6 sp] 3 times, ch 5, sk next sc, sk next ch-4 sp, tr in next 2 tr; repeat from * to last 2 tr, tr2tog (working in next tr and top of turning ch).
Row 14 Ch 4, turn, tr in next 2 tr, ch 6, sk next ch-5 sp, sk next sc, sc in next ch-6 sp, [ch 6, sk next sc, sc in next ch-6 sp] twice, ch 6, sk next sc, sk next ch-5 sp, *tr in next 5 tr, ch 6, sk next ch-5 sp, sk next sc, sc in next ch-6 sp, [ch 6, sk next sc, sc in next ch-6 sp] twice, ch 6, sk next sc, sk next ch-5 sp; repeat from * across to last 3 tr, tr in last 3 tr (last tr is turning ch).
Row 15 Ch 4, turn, tr in next 2 tr, ch 7, sk next ch-6 sp, sk next sc, sc in next ch-6 sp, ch 6, sk next sc, sc in next ch-6 sp, ch 7, sk next sc, sk next ch-6 sp, *tr in next 5 tr, ch 7, sk next ch-6 sp, sk next sc, sc in next ch-6 sp, ch 6, sk next sc, sc in next ch-6 sp, ch 7, sk next sc, sk next ch-6 sp; repeat from * across to last 3 tr, tr in last 3 tr (last tr in turning ch).
Row 16 Ch 7, turn, tr in first 3 tr, ch 8, sk next ch-7 sp, sk next sc, sc in next ch-6 sp, ch 8, sk next sc, sk next ch-7 sp, tr in next 2 tr, *[tr, ch 5, tr] in next tr, tr in next 2 tr, ch 8, sk next ch-7 sp, sk next sc, sc in next ch-6 sp, ch 8, sk next sc, sk next ch-7 sp, tr in next 2 tr; repeat from * across to last tr (turning ch), [tr, ch 3, tr] in last tr.
Row 17 Ch 6 (counts as dtr, ch 1), tr in first ch-3 sp, ch 3, tr in next 3 tr, ch 7, sk next 2 ch-8 sps, tr in next 3 tr, *ch 3, [tr, ch 3, tr] in next ch-5 sp, ch 3, tr in next 3 tr, ch 7, sk next 2 ch-8 sps ch, tr in next 3 tr; repeat from * across to turning ch, ch 3, sk next 3 ch of turning ch, [tr, ch 1, dtr] in next ch.
Repeat Rows 2–17 for Pattern.

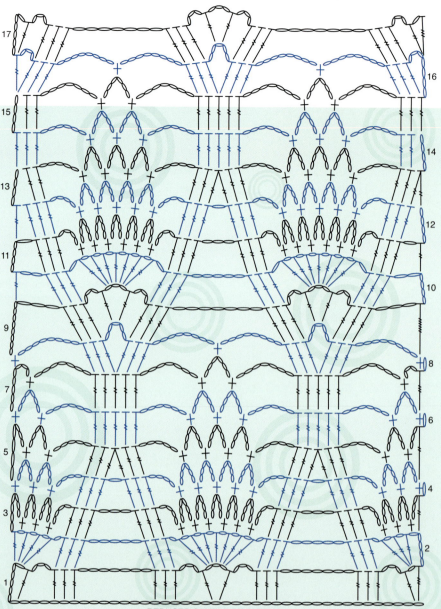

REDUCED SAMPLE OF PATTERN

Front & Back
(make 2 the same)
Ch 127 (147, 167).
Row 1 Work Pat St Row 1–6 (7, 8) pattern repeats.
Rows 2–17 Work Pat St Rows 2–17.
Rows 18–28 Work Pat St Rows 2–12.

Shape armhole
Row 1 Ch 1, turn, sk first tr, sl st in next 2 tr, sc in next tr, ch 3, sk next ch-4 sp, sk next sc, sc in next ch-6 sp, [ch 6, sk next sc, sc in next ch-6 sp] 3 times, *ch 5, sk next sc, sk next ch-4 sp, tr in next 2 tr, tr2tog (sk ch-1 sp between the next 2 tr when working the tr2tog), tr in next 2 tr, ch 5, sk next ch-4 sp, sk next sc, sc in next ch-6 sp, [ch 6, sk next sc, sc in next ch-6 sp] 3 times; repeat from * to last ch-4 sp, ch 3, sk last ch-4 sp, sc in next tr, sl st in next tr; leave rem sts unworked.
Row 2 Turn, sl st to center ch of first ch-6 sp, [ch 6, sk next sc, sc in next ch-6 sp] twice, ch 6, sk next sc, sk next ch-5 sp, tr in next 5 tr, ch 6, sk next ch-5 sp, sk next sc, sc in

lacy Pineapples

next ch-6 sp, [ch 6, sk next sc, sc in next ch-6 sp] twice, *ch 6, sk next sc, sk next ch-5 sp, tr in next 5 tr, ch 6, sk next ch-5 sp, sk next sc, sc in next ch-6 sp, [ch 6, sk next sc, sc in next ch-6 sp] twice; repeat from * across to last ch-3 sp; leave rem sts unworked.
Row 3 Turn, sl st to center ch of first ch-6 sp, ch 7, sk next sc, sc in next ch-6 sp, ch 7, sk next sc, sk next ch-6 sp, tr in next 5 tr, ch 7, sk next ch-6 sp, sk next sc, sc in next ch-6 sp, *ch 6, sk next sc, sc in next ch-6 sp, ch 7, sk next sc, sk next ch-6 sp, tr in next 5 tr, ch 7, sk next ch-6 sp, sk next sc, sc in next ch-6 sp; repeat from * across to last ch-6 sp, ch 3, tr in last ch-6 sp—5 (6, 7) repeats.

Size 2X/3X only
Row 4 Turn, sl st to center ch of first ch-7 sp, ch 4, tr in next 2 tr, [tr, ch 5, tr] in next tr, tr in next 2 tr, *ch 8, sk next ch-7 sp, sk next sc, sc in next ch-6 sp, ch 8, sk next sc, sk next ch-7 sp, tr in next 2 tr, [tr, ch 5, tr] in next tr, tr in next 2 tr; repeat from * to last ch-7 sp, tr in center ch of last ch-7 sp; leave rem sts unworked.
Row 5 Turn, sl st in next 3 tr, ch 6 (counts as dtr, ch 1), tr in next ch-5 sp, ch 3, tr in next 3 tr, *ch 7, sk next 2 ch-8 sps, tr in next 3 tr, ch 3, *[tr, ch 3, tr] in next ch-5 sp, ch 3, tr in next 3 tr, ch 7, sk next 2 ch-8 sps, tr in next 3 tr, ch 3; repeat from * to last ch-5 sp, [tr, ch 1, dtr] in last ch-5 sp; leave rem sts unworked—6 repeats.
Beginning with Row 8 (8, 2) of Pat St, work even in Pat St until piece measures 23 (23½, 24)"/ 58.5 (59.5, 61)cm from beginning.
Fasten off.

Finishing
Mark center 10"/25.5cm of top edge of front and back. Working from wrong side, sew shoulder seams leaving center 10"/25.5cm open for neck. Working from wrong side, sew side seams, leaving 5"/12.5cm open at each lower edge (for side slit).

Lower edging
With right side facing, join yarn with sl st in side seam of lower edge (at slit).
Rnd 1 Ch 1, working in ends of rows and free loops on opposite side of foundation ch, sc evenly spaced around lower edge, work 3 sc in each corner, and work sc2tog at the top of each side slit; join with sl st in first sc.
Rnd 2 Ch 1, sc in each sc around, work 3 sc in each corner, and work sc2tog at the top of each side slit; join with sl st in first sc. Fasten off.

Neck edging
With right side facing, join yarn with sl st in shoulder seam.
Rnd 1 Ch 1, work sc evenly spaced around neck edge; join with sl st in first sc.
Rnd 2 Ch 1, sc in each sc around; join with sl st in first sc. Fasten off.

Armhole edging
With right side facing, join yarn with sl st in side seam at armhole.
Rnd 1 Ch 1, work sc evenly spaced around armhole edge; join with sl st in first sc.
Rnd 2 Ch 1, sc in each sc around; join with sl st in first sc. Fasten off.
Repeat on other armhole.
Weave in all ends.

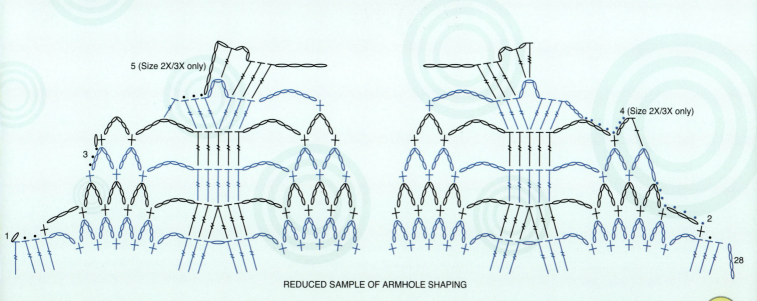

REDUCED SAMPLE OF ARMHOLE SHAPING

Yarn
AUNT LYDIA'S *Fashion Crochet Thread*, Size 3, each ball approx 150yd/137m (cotton)
7 (7, 8, 9, 10, 12) balls #0926 Bridal White

Crochet Hooks
Size D/3 (3.25mm) crochet hook *or size to obtain gauge*

Notions
Stitch markers
3 (3, 4, 4, 5) buttons, ¾"/19mm diameter
Yarn needle

Basic stitches and a simple silhouette make a big impact in this sweet sweater. Top off your warm-weather look with this light and lovely layering piece.

TIP: Customize it! For more coverage, adjust the length of the bodice by working additional rows in double crochet, without increasing. Adjust the length of the skirt by repeating Rows 20 and 21 more or fewer times.

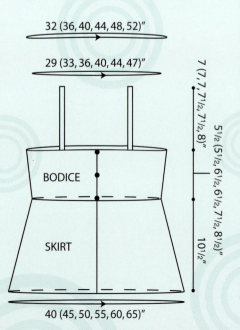

Sizes
XS (S, M, L, 1X, 2X)

Finished Measurements
Chest 32 (36, 40, 44, 48, 52)"/81.5 (91.5, 101.5, 111.5, 122, 132)cm
Length 23 (23, 24, 24½, 25½, 26)"/58.5 (58.5, 61, 62, 65, 66)cm

Gauge
25 dc and 12 rows = 4"/10cm using size D/3 (3.25mm) crochet hook.
Take time to check gauge.

Note
Bodice of Tank Top is crocheted first, from the lower edge to the top edge. The skirt is then worked from the lower edge of the bodice down to the hem.

Bodice
Beginning at lower edge of bodice, ch 187 (211, 232, 256, 277, 298).
Row 1 (right side) Dc in 4th ch from hook (beginning ch counts as first dc) and in each remaining ch across—185 (209, 230, 254, 275, 296) dc.

botanical Babydoll

Rows 2 and 3 Ch 3 (counts as first dc here and throughout), turn, dc in each st across.
Row 4 Ch 3, turn, dc in next 43 (49, 54, 60, 65, 70) sts, 2 dc in next st, dc in next st, place marker in last st made, 2 dc in next st, dc in next 91 (103, 114, 126, 137, 148) sts, 2 dc in next st, dc in next st, place marker in last st made, 2 dc in next st, dc in last 44 (50, 55, 61, 66, 71) sts—189 (213, 234, 258, 279, 300) dc.
Move markers up as work proceeds.
Rows 5 and 6 Ch 3, turn, dc in each st across.
Row 7 Ch 3, turn, dc in each st to 1 st before marker, 2 dc in next st, dc in next st (marked), 2 dc in next st, dc in each st to 1 st before next marker, 2 dc in next st, dc in next st (marked), 2 dc in next st, dc in each st to end—193 (217, 238, 262, 283, 304) dc.
Rows 8–16 (16, 19, 19, 22, 25) Repeat Rows 5–7, 3 (3, 4, 4, 5, 6) times—205 (229, 254, 278, 303, 328) dc.
Row 17 (17, 20, 20, 23, 26) Ch 3, turn, dc in each st across. Fasten off.

Skirt

With right side facing, join thread with sl st in first ch along opposite side of foundation ch (at lower left edge of bodice).
Row 1 Working along opposite side of foundation ch, ch 1, sc in same ch, ch 5, sk next ch, sc in next ch, *ch 5, sk next 2 ch, sc in next ch; repeat from * across to last 2 ch, ch 5, sk next ch, sc in last ch (base of beginning ch)—62 (70, 77, 85, 92, 99) ch-5 spaces, and 63 (71, 78, 86, 93, 100) sc.
Row 2 Ch 5 (counts as dc, ch 2), turn, sc in first ch-5 space, *ch 5, sc in next ch-5 space; repeat from * across, ch 2, dc in last sc.
Row 3 Ch 1, turn, sc in first dc, *ch 5, sc in next ch-5 space; repeat from * to turning ch, ch 5, sc in 3rd ch of turning ch.
Rows 4–17 Repeat Rows 2 and 3 seven times.

Row 18 Repeat Row 2.
Row 19 Ch 1, turn, sc in first dc, *ch 6, sc in next ch-5 space; repeat from * to turning ch, ch 6, sc in 3rd ch of turning ch—62 (70, 77, 85, 92, 99) ch-6 spaces, and 63 (71, 78, 86, 93, 100) sc.
Row 20 Ch 7 (counts as tr, ch 3), turn, sc in first ch-6 space, *ch 6, sc in next ch-6 space; repeat from * across, ch 3, tr in last sc.
Row 21 Ch 1, turn, sc in first tr, *ch 6, sc in next ch-6 space; repeat from * to turning ch, ch 6, sc in 4th ch of turning ch.
Rows 22–35 Repeat Rows 20 and 21 seven times. Fasten off.

Strap (make 2)

Ch 92 (92, 92, 98, 98, 104).
Rnd 1 Sc in 2nd ch from hook, *ch 1, sk next ch, sc in next ch; repeat from * across; pivot to work along opposite side of foundation ch, ch 1, sl st in same ch (at base of last sc made), *ch 1, sk next ch, sl st in next ch; repeat from * across; ch 1; join with sl st in first sc. Fasten off.

Finishing

Edging

Place 3 (3, 4, 4, 4, 5) markers evenly spaced along right front edge of bodice (for buttonholes). With right side facing, join thread with sl st in lower right front corner.
Row 1 Ch 1, working in ends of rows of right front edge, sc in same space, *work [ch 1, sc in edge] evenly spaced to buttonhole marker; ch 5, sk next row of bodice, sc in end of next row; repeat from * 2 (2, 3, 3, 3, 4) more times; **ch 1, sc in edge; repeat from ** working evenly spaced to top of bodice, across top of bodice, and down left front edge to lower left front corner. Fasten off.
Sew buttons opposite buttonholes.
Sew straps inside top edge of bodice, spaced approx 7"/18cm apart on the back and front. Before sewing straps, adjust strap placement to achieve the desired bodice height and armhole depth.
Weave in all ends.

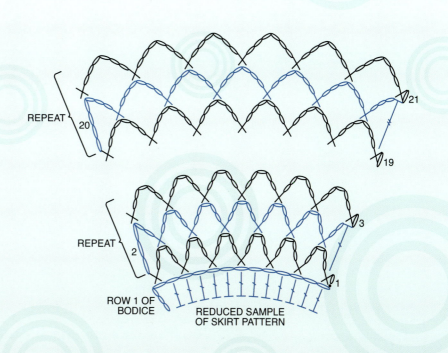

REPEAT
ROW 1 OF BODICE
REDUCED SAMPLE OF SKIRT PATTERN

romantic Wrap

Yarn
AUNT LYDIA'S *Bamboo Crochet Thread*, Size 10, each ball approx 300yd/274m (viscose from bamboo)
6 balls #226 Natural

Crochet Hooks
Size 0 (3.25mm) steel crochet hook *or size to obtain gauge*

Notions
Yarn needle

Stitched in a soft bamboo thread, this lacy wrap drapes and flows beautifully. It's the perfect accessory for dressy garden parties and weddings.

Stitch Glossary
picot Ch 3, sl st in 3rd ch from hook.

Tip
Go wide! Simply repeat Rows 3–5 a few more times on each half of wrap. You may need more thread than the pattern requires to make the wrap wider.

Finished Measurements
Wrap measures approx 60"/152.5cm long x 11½"/29cm wide

Gauge
2 pattern repeats = 5"/12.5cm; Rows 1–3 = 1½"/4cm; worked with 2 strands of thread held tog.
Take time to check gauge.

How to Make a Gauge Swatch
Note Diagram shows reduced sample of wrap pattern and differs from swatch instructions.
With 2 strands of thread held tog, ch 32.
Row 1 Sc in 2nd ch from hook; *ch 6, sk next 4 chs, sc in next ch; repeat from * across—6 ch-6 sps.
Row 2 Ch 7 (counts as tr and ch-3 sp), turn, sc in next ch-6 sp, 8 tr in next ch-6 sp, sc in next ch-6 sp, ch 6, sc in next ch-6 sp, 8 tr in next ch-6 sp, sc in next ch-6 sp; ch 3, tr in last sc—2 pattern repeats consisting of 2 8-tr groups, 1 ch-6 sp, 2 ch-3 sps, and 2 tr.
Row 3 Ch 1, turn, sc in first tr, [tr in next tr, picot] 7 times, tr in next tr, sc in next ch-6 sp, [tr in next tr, picot] 7 times, tr in next tr, sc in last tr.
Resulting gauge swatch should measure approx 5"/12.5cm long x 1½"/4cm wide.
Adjust hook size if necessary to obtain correct gauge.

Wrap
First half
With 2 strands of thread held tog, ch 372.
Row 1 (wrong side) Sc in 2nd ch from hook, *ch 6, sk next 4 ch, sc in next ch; repeat from * across to last 5 ch, ch 3, sk next 4 ch, dc in last ch (last ch-3 and dc count as last ch-6 sp here and throughout)—74 ch-6 sp.
Row 2 Ch 1, turn, sc in first ch-6 sp, *ch 6, sc in next ch-6 sp, 8 tr in next ch-6 sp, sc in next ch-6 sp; repeat from * across, ch 3, dc in last ch-6 sp—24 pattern repeats consisting of 24 8-tr groups and 25 ch-6 sps.
Row 3 Ch 1, turn, sc in first ch-6 sp, *[tr in next tr, picot] 7 times, tr in next tr, sc in next ch-6 sp; repeat from * across.
Row 4 Turn, [ch 6, sk next picot, sc in next picot] 3 times, *ch 6, sk next 2 picots, sc in next picot, [ch 6, sk next picot, sc in next picot] twice; repeat from * across, ch 3, sk last picot, dc in last sc—73 ch-6 sps.
Row 5 Turn; sl st in next 3 ch, sl st in next sc, sl st in next 3 ch of next ch-6 sp, ch 1, sc in same ch-6 sp, *ch 6, sc in next ch-6 sp, 8 tr in next ch-6 sp, sc in next ch-6 sp; repeat from * across to last 2 ch-6 sps, ch 3, dc in next ch-6 sp, leave last ch-6 sp unworked—23 pattern repeats.
Rows 6–11 Repeat Rows 3–5 twice—21 pattern repeats.
Row 12 Repeat Row 3. Fasten off.

Second half
Row 13 With right side facing and working in ch-4 sps along opposite side of foundation ch, hold 2 strands of thread tog and join thread with sc in first ch-4 sp, *ch 6, sc in next ch-4 sp, 8 tr in next ch-4 sp, sc in next ch-4 sp; repeat from * across to last ch-4 sp, ch 3, dc in last ch-4 sp—24 pattern repeats.
Rows 14–23 Repeat Rows 3–12.

Finishing
Weave in all ends.

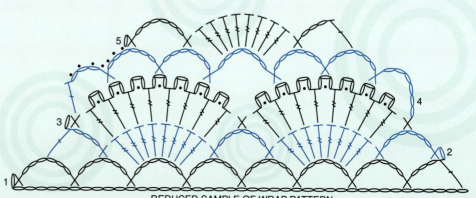

REDUCED SAMPLE OF WRAP PATTERN

Yarn

AUNT LYDIA'S *Bamboo Crochet Thread*, Size 10, each ball approx. 300yd/274m (viscose from bamboo)
3 (4, 5) balls #320 Mushroom (A)
1 (2, 2) balls #226 Natural (B)
1 (2, 2) balls #810 Blue (C)

Crochet Hooks

Size 8 (1.5mm) steel crochet hook *or size to obtain gauge*

Notions

Stitch markers
5 buttons ¾"/19mm diameter
Thread needle

Add a little vintage charm to your wardrobe with this amazingly light and silky vest. Fine bamboo thread creates a delicate fabric, and join-as-you-go construction helps the whole piece come together surprisingly quickly. By Kazekobo

Stitch Glossary

Beg-Cl (beginning cluster) Ch 3, yarn over, insert hook in indicated sp, yarn over and draw up a loop, yarn over and draw through 2 loops on hook; yarn over, insert hook in same sp, yarn over and draw up a loop, yarn over and draw through 2 loops on hook, yarn over and draw through all 3 loops on hook.

Cl (cluster) Yarn over, insert hook in indicated sp, yarn over and draw up a loop, yarn over and draw through 2 loops on hook; [yarn over, insert hook in same sp, yarn over and draw up a loop, yarn over and draw through 2 loops on hook] twice, yarn over and draw through all 4 loops on hook.

Sizes

S/M (L, 1X/2X)
Finished chest 36 (42, 48)"/91.5 (106.5, 122)cm, excluding body edging
Finished length 21 (24½, 28)"/53.5 (62, 71)cm

Gauge

Rounds 1–5 of square motif = 3 x 3"/7.5 x 7.5cm;
Take time to check gauge.

How to Make a Gauge Swatch
Work Rounds 1–5 of square motif. Resulting motif should measure approx 3 x 3"/7.5 x 7.5cm. If necessary, adjust hook size to obtain correct gauge.

Notes

1 Motifs are worked and joined as you go.
2 Refer to the assembly diagram for motif placement. Motifs can be made and joined in any order desired (alternating motifs of different color sequences). The numbers on the assembly diagram provide a suggested order for joining motifs.

Square Motif

(make 66—33 in each color sequence)
Color sequence #1 B, C, A
Color sequence #2 C, B, A
With first color in sequence, ch 4; join with sl st in first ch to form a ring.
Round 1 Ch 4 (counts as dc, ch 1), [dc in ring, ch 1] 11 times; join with sl st in 3rd ch of beginning ch—12 dc and 12 ch-1 sps.
Round 2 (Sl st, Beg-Cl) in first ch-1 sp, ch 3, [Cl in next ch-1 sp, ch 3] 11 times; join with sl st in first cluster—12 clusters and 12 ch-3 sps. Fasten off.
Round 3 Join 2nd color in sequence with sl st in any ch-3 sp, ch 3, 2 dc in same ch-3 sp, [ch 3, 3 dc in next ch-3 sp] 11 times; join with ch 1, hdc in top of beginning ch (join counts as first ch-3 sp)—36 dc and 12 ch-3 sps.
Round 4 Ch 1, sc in first ch-3 sp (formed by join), ch 6, sc in next ch-3 sp, ch 9 (corner made), *sc in next

light as air Vest

ch-3 sp, [ch 6, sc in next ch-3 sp] twice, ch 9; repeat from * 2 more times, sc in next ch-3 sp, ch 6; join with sl st in first sc—8 ch-6 sps and 4 corner ch-9 sps. Fasten off.
Round 5 Join 3rd color with sl st in last ch-6 sp made, ch 5 (counts as dc, ch 2), 4 dc in next ch-6 sp, ch 2, (4 dc, ch 5, 4 dc) in corner ch-9 sp, *[ch 2, 4 dc in next ch-6 sp] twice, ch 2, (4 dc, ch 5, 4 dc) in corner ch-9 sp; repeat from * 2 more times, ch 2, 3 dc in same ch-6 sp as join; join with sl st in 3rd ch of beginning ch—64 dc (consisting of four 4-dc groups across each side), 12 ch-2 sps (consisting of 3 ch-2 sps across each side), and 4 corner ch-5 sps.

Sizes L (1X/2X) only
Round 6 Sl st in each st to first ch-sp, (sl st, ch 3, 3 dc) in first ch-sp, ch 3, 4 dc in next ch-sp, ch 3, (4 dc, ch 5, 4 dc) in corner ch-5 sp, [ch 3, *4 dc in next ch-sp, ch 3; repeat from * to next corner ch-5 sp, (4 dc, ch 5, 4 dc) in corner ch-5 sp] 3 times, ch 3, **4 dc in next ch-sp, ch 3; repeat from ** around; join with sl st in top of beginning ch—80 (96) dc (consisting of five (six) 4-dc groups across each side), 16 (20) ch-3 sps (consisting of 4 (5) ch-sps across each side), and 4 corner ch-5 sps.

Size 1X/2X only
Round 7 Repeat Round 6.

All Sizes
Note Work Last Round of first square motif without any joins. For all remaining motifs, join to neighboring motif(s) as you go. Refer to assembly diagram to determine placement of motif, while working Last Round, join as follows:
Ch-3 side join To join side ch-3 sp to corresponding ch-3 sp of neighboring motif; work ch 1, sl st in corresponding ch-3 sp of neighboring motif, ch 1.
Ch-5 corner join To join corner ch-5 sp to corresponding corner ch-sp of neighboring motif; work ch 2, sl st in corresponding corner ch-sp of neighboring motif, ch 2.
Last Round (joining round) Sl st in each st to first ch-sp, (sl st, ch 3, 3 dc) in first ch-2 sp, ch 3 or ch-3 side join, 4 dc in next ch-sp, ch 3 or ch-3 side join, (4 dc, ch 5 or ch-5 corner join, 4 dc) in corner ch-5 sp, [ch 3 or ch-3 side join, *4 dc in next ch-sp, ch 3 or ch-3 side join; repeat from * to next corner ch-5 sp, (4 dc, ch 5 or ch-5 corner join, 4 dc) in corner

HALF MOTIF (SIZE 1X/2X)

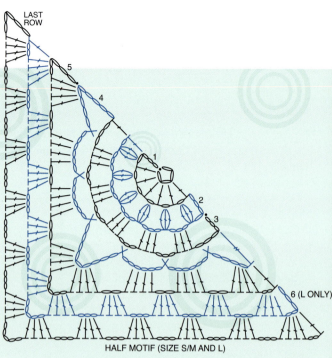
HALF MOTIF (SIZE S/M AND L)

ch-5 sp] 3 times, ch 3 or ch-3 side join, **4 dc in next ch-sp, ch 3 or ch-3 side join; repeat from ** around; join with sl st in top of beginning ch. Fasten off.

Half Motif
(make 6—3 in each color sequence)
With first color, ch 4; join with sl st in first ch to form a ring.
Row 1 (right side) Ch 4 (counts as dc, ch 1 here and throughout), dc in ring, [ch 1, dc in ring] 5 times—7 dc and 7 ch-1 sps.
Row 2 Ch 4, turn, Cl in next ch-1 sp, [ch 2, Cl in next ch-1 sp] 5 times, ch 1, dc in 3rd ch of turning ch—6 clusters, 5 ch-2 sps, and 2 ch-1 sps. Fasten off.
Row 3 (wrong side) With wrong side facing, join 2nd color with sl st in 3rd ch of beginning ch of Row 2, ch 6 (counts as dc, ch 3), sk first ch-1 sp, 3 dc in next ch-2 sp, ch 3, [3 dc in next ch-2 sp, ch 3] 4 times, sk last ch-1 sp, dc in last dc—17 dc, and 6 ch-3 sps.
Row 4 Ch 9 (counts as tr, ch 4), turn, sc in first ch-3 sp, [ch 6, sc in next ch-3 sp] twice, ch 9 (corner made), sc in next ch-3 sp, [ch 6, sc in next ch-3 sp] twice, ch 4, tr in 3rd ch of turning ch—2 ch-4 sps, 4 ch-6 sps, and 1 corner ch-9 sp. Fasten off.
Row 5 (right side) With right side facing, join 3rd color with sl st in 5th ch of beginning ch of Row 4, ch 5 (counts

as dc, ch 2), 4 dc in first ch-4 sp, [ch 2, 4 dc in next ch-6 sp] twice, ch 2, (4 dc, ch 5, 4 dc) in corner ch-9 sp, [ch 2, 4 dc in next ch-6 sp] twice, ch 2, 4 dc, in last ch-4 sp, ch 2, dc in tr—32 dc (consisting of four 4-dc groups across each side), 8 ch-2 sps (consisting of 4 ch-2 sps across each side), and 1 corner ch-5 sp.

Size L only
Row 6 Ch 5 (counts as dc, ch 2), turn, *4 dc in next ch-sp, ch 3; repeat from * across to corner ch-5 sp, (4 dc, ch 5, 4 dc) in corner ch-9 sp, **ch 3, 4 dc in next ch-sp; repeat from ** across, ch 2, dc in 3rd ch of turning ch—40 dc (consisting of five 4-dc groups across each side), 8 ch-3 sps (consisting of 4 ch-3 sps across each side), 2 ch-2 sps, and 1 corner ch-5 sp.

Size (1X/2X) only
Row 6 Ch 3 (counts as dc), turn, 2 dc in first ch-sp, ch 3, *4 dc in next ch-sp, ch 3; repeat from * across to corner ch-5 sp, (4 dc, ch 5, 4 dc) in corner ch-9 sp, **ch 3, 4 dc in next ch-sp; repeat from ** across to last ch-sp, ch 3, 2 dc in last ch-sp, dc in 3rd ch of turning ch—38 dc (consisting of four 4-dc groups and one 3-dc group across each side), 8 ch-3 sps (consisting of 4 ch-3 sps across each side),

and 1 corner ch-5 sp.
Row 7 Ch 8 (counts as dc, ch 5), turn, *4 dc in next ch-sp, ch 3; repeat from * across to corner ch-5 sp, (4 dc, ch 5, 4 dc) in corner ch-9 sp, **ch 3, 4 dc in next ch-sp; repeat from ** across, ch 5, dc in top of turning ch—40 dc (consisting of five 4-dc groups across each side), 8 ch-3 sps (consisting of 4 ch-3 sps across each side), 1 ch-5 sp at each end, and 1 corner ch-5 sp.

Refer to assembly diagram to determine placement of motif, join two sides of half motif to any neighboring motifs in same manner as joining square motifs.

Last Row (joining row) Turn, ch 5 or ch-5 corner join, *4 dc in next ch-sp, ch 3 or ch-3 side join; repeat from * across to corner ch-5 sp, (4 dc, ch 5 or ch-5 corner join, 4 dc) in corner ch-5 sp, **ch 3 or ch-3 side join, 4 dc in next ch-sp; repeat from ** across, ch 2, dc in 3rd ch of turning ch. Fasten off.

Finishing
Weave in all ends.

Body edging
Round 1 With right side facing, join A with sc in lower front ch-5 sp, work 2 more sc in same ch-5 sp, work sc in

light as air Vest

each st along front edge, across back neck, down opposite front edge, work 7 sc in lower front corner ch-5 sp, sc in each st along remainder of lower edge, 4 sc in same ch-5 sp as join; join with sl st in first sc.
Place 5 stitch markers evenly spaced along right front edge (for buttonhole placement)
Round 2 (buttonhole round) Ch 1, turn, (sc, ch 1, sc) in first sc (corner), ch 1, *sk next sc, sc in next sc, ch 1; repeat from * across to next lower edge corner, (sc, ch 1, sc) in corner sc; [**ch 1, sk next sc, sc in next sc; repeat from ** to next buttonhole marker, ch 5, sk next 5 sc, sc in next sc] 5 times; ch 1, ***sk next sc, sc in next sc, ch 1; repeat from *** around; join with sl st in first sc.
Round 3 Ch 1, turn, sc in first ch-1 sp, ch 1, *sk next sc, sc in next ch-1 sp, ch 1; repeat from * around, working (sc, ch 1, sc, ch 1) in each lower edge corner ch-1 sp and each front neck corner ch-1 sp, and working (sc, ch 1, sc, ch 1, sc, ch 1) in each ch-5 buttonhole; join with sl st in first sc.
Round 4 Ch 1, turn, sc in first ch-1 sp, ch 1, *sk next sc, sc in next ch-1 sp, ch 1; repeat from * around, working (sc, ch 1, sc, ch 1) in each lower edge corner ch-1 sp (do not work (sc, ch 1, sc) in front neck corner ch-1 sp); join with sl st in first sc.

Round 5 (picot round) Ch 1, turn, sc in first ch-1 sp, *ch 1, sk next sc, sc in next ch-1 sp, ch 4, sl st in top of last sc made, ch 1, sk next sc, sc in next ch-1 sp; repeat from * around; join with sl st in first sc. Fasten off.

Armhole edging
Round 1 With right side facing, join A with sc at underarm, work sc in each st around armhole; join with sl st in first sc.
Round 2 Ch 1, turn, sc in first sc, ch 1, *sk next sc, sc in next sc, ch 1; repeat from * around; join with sl st in first sc.
Rounds 3 and 4 Ch 1, turn, sc in first ch-1 sp, ch 1, *sk next sc, sc in next ch-1 sp, ch 1; repeat from * around; join with sl st in first sc.
Round 5 (picot round) Work Round 5 of body edging. Fasten off.

Repeat around other armhole.

Weave in all ends.

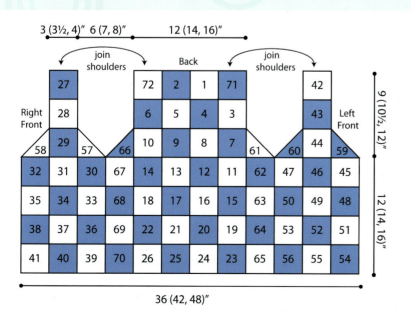

Half Motif in Color Sequence #1
Half Motif in Color Sequence #2
Square Motif in Color Sequence #1
Square Motif in Color Sequence #2

Motifs can be made and joined in any order desired. The numbers on the diagram suggest a joining order.

mixed motif Cami

Yarn
AUNT LYDIA'S *Fashion Crochet Thread*, Size 3, approx 150yd/137m each ball (mercerized cotton)
3 (3, 3, 4, 4, 4, 5) balls #871 Plum (A)
1 ball #377 Tan (B)
Note Yarn quantities may differ depending on which and the number of motifs you choose to make.

Crochet Hooks
Size E/4 (3.5 mm) crochet hook *or size to obtain gauge*

Notions
25 x 60"/63.5 x 152.5cm piece of lightweight paper or fabric
Thin leather cord for straps
Yarn needle

Lacy shapes are collaged together in this stunning tank. Create a top just like ours, or design your own arrangement with our easy-to-use pattern.

Sizes
XS (S, M, L, 1X, 2X, 3X)

Finished Measurements
Bust: 30 (34, 38, 42, 46, 50, 54)"/76 (86.5, 96.5, 106.5, 116.5, 127, 137)cm
Length: 20 (20, 20½, 21½, 22, 22½, 23)"/51 (51, 52, 53.5, 56, 57, 58.5)cm

Gauge
Large circle motif = 4"/10cm using size E/4 (3.5mm) crochet hook.
Take time to check gauge.

Stitch Glossary
begCl (beginning cluster) Ch 3 (counts as first dc), [yo, insert hook in same st, yo and draw up a loop, yo and draw through 2 loops on hook] twice, yo and draw through all 3 loops on hook.
Cl (cluster) Yo, insert hook in next ch-1 sp, yo and draw up a loop, yo and draw through 2 loops on hook, [yo, insert hook in same ch-sp, yo and draw up a loop, yo and draw through 2 loops on hook] twice, yo and draw through all 4 loops on hook.
FPhdc (Front Post half double crochet) Yo, insert hook from front to back to front around post of indicated stitch; yo and draw up a loop, yo and draw through all 3 loops on hook. Skip stitch behind FPhdc.

Note
1 Shell consists of two identically shaped pieces, front and back. Each piece is made by crocheting any number of motifs, arranging the motifs within an outline of the shape of the piece, and joining the motifs with a mesh of chain spaces and slip stitches.
2 Make as many motifs of each type as desired. You need enough motifs to fill the outline of the front and back pieces, leaving only a little space between motifs.
3 The assembly diagram shows how the motifs were arranged in our model garment which is size M.

Create Outline
On lightweight paper or fabric, draw a life-sized outline (one for front and one for back piece) of the schematic with your desired measurements. As you crochet, place completed motifs within the outlines arranging them any way you like until the outlines are filled. Leave only enough space between motifs to ensure correct size and shape of each piece.

Large Circle Motif
(make as many as desired)
With A, ch 5; join with sl st in first ch to form a ring.
Rnd 1 Sl st in ring, ch 4 (counts as dc, ch 1), [dc in ring, ch 1] 11 times; join with sl st in 3rd ch of beginning ch-4—12 ch-1 sp.
Rnd 2 Sl st in first ch-1 sp, begCl in same ch-sp, ch 3, [Cl in next ch-sp, ch 3] around; join with sl st in top of begCl—12 clusters.
Rnd 3 Sl st in first ch-3 sp, ch 3 (counts as dc), 4 dc in same ch-sp, ch 1, [5 dc in next ch-3 sp, ch 1] around; join with sl st in top of beginning ch-3—12 dc-groups.
Rnd 4 Ch 4 (counts as dc, ch 1), sk 1 dc, FPhdc around next dc, ch 1, sk 1 dc, hdc in next dc, ch 1, [dc in next dc, ch 1, sk 1 dc, FPhdc around next dc, ch 1, sk 1 dc, hdc in next dc, ch 1] around; join with sl st in 2nd ch of beginning ch-3. Fasten off.

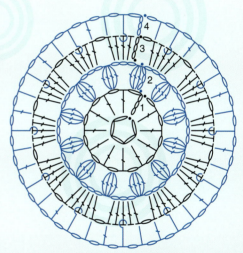

LARGE CIRCLE MOTIF

Medium Circle Motif
(make as many as desired)
With A, ch 5; join with sl st in first ch to form a ring.
Rnd 1 Sl st in ring, ch 3 (counts as dc), work 23 dc in ring; join with sl st in top of beginning ch-3—24 dc.
Rnd 2 Ch 2 (counts as hdc), hdc in same st, ch 1, sk 1 dc, [2 hdc in next dc, ch 1, sk 1 dc] around; join with sl st in top of beginning ch-2—24 hdc.
Rnd 3 Turn, sl st in next ch-1 sp, sl st in next hdc, ch 3 (counts as dc), 2 dc in same st, ch 1, sk 1 hdc, [sk next ch-1 sp, 3 dc in next hdc, ch 1, sk 1 hdc] around; join with sl st in top of beginning ch 3. Fasten off.

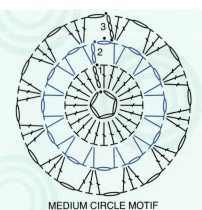

MEDIUM CIRCLE MOTIF

Small Circle Motif
(make as many as desired)
Work as for Large Circle Motif through Rnd 1. Fasten off.

Pineapple Motif
(make as many as desired)
With A, ch 6; join with sl st in first ch to form a ring.
Row 1 Ch 3 (counts as dc), work 12 dc in ring; do not join—13 dc.

SMALL CIRCLE MOTIF

Row 2 Ch 3 (counts as hdc, ch 1), turn, hdc in next dc, [ch 1, hdc in next dc] across—12 ch-1 sp.
Row 3 Ch 1, turn, sc in first ch-1 sp, [ch 1, sc in next ch-1 sp] across—11 ch-1 sp.
Rows 4–13 Repeat Row 3, working one less ch-1 sp in each row until there is only 1 ch-1 sp rem.
Row 14 Turn, sl st in ch-1 sp. Fasten off.

Large Square
(make as many as desired)
With B, ch 5; join with sl st in first ch to form a ring.
Rnd 1 Ch 1, sc in ring, [ch 8, sc in ring] 7 times, ch 3, tr in ring (ch 3 and tr count as 8th ch-sp)—8 ch-sps.
Rnd 2 [Ch 6, sc in next ch-8 sp] 7 times, ch 2, tr in last tr (ch 2 and tr count as 8th ch-sp).
Rnd 3 Ch 3 (counts as dc), 6 dc in same ch-sp (formed by ch 2 and tr), [7 dc in next ch-sp] 7 times; join with sl st in top of beginning ch-3. Fasten off B.
Rnd 4 Join A with sl st in first dc of any 7-dc group, ch 1, sc in same st, [ch 1, sk 1 dc, sc in next dc] 3 times, ch 1, * sc in first dc of next 7-dc group, [ch 1, sk 1 dc, sc in next dc] 3 times, ch 1; repeat from * around; join with sl st in first sc—32 ch-1 sp.
Rnd 5 Sl st in first ch-1 sp, ch 1, sc in same sp, [ch 1, sk 1 sc, sc in next ch-1 sp] 3 times, ch 1, sc in same ch-1 sp,

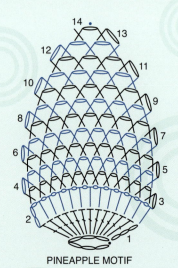

PINEAPPLE MOTIF

* [ch 1, sk 1 sc, sc in next ch-1 sp] 4 times, ch 1, sc in same ch-1 sp; repeat

from * around to last sc, ch 1, sk last sc; join with sl st in first sc—40 ch-1 sp.
Rnd 6 Sl st in first ch-1 sp, ch 1, sc in same sp, ch 1, sk 1 sc, [sc in next ch-1 sp, ch 1, sk 1 sc] around; join with sl st in first sc. Fasten off A.
Rnd 7 Join B in any ch-1 sp, ch 1, sc in same sp, ch 3, sk 1 sc, [dc in next ch-1 sp, ch 3, sk 1 sc, sc in next ch-1 sp, ch 3, sk 1 sc] around to last ch-1 sp, yo and insert hook in next ch-1 sp, yo and draw up a loop, yo and draw through 2 loops on hook, yo and insert hook in first ch-1 sp (to join), yo and draw up loop, yo and draw through 2 loops on hook, yo and draw through all 3 loops on hook—20 dc.
Rnd 8 [Ch 7, sc in next dc] 19 times, ch 1, dtr in base of beginning ch-7 (ch 1, dtr counts as 20th ch-sp)—20 ch-sp.
Rnd 9 Ch 3 (counts as dc), 6 dc in same ch-sp (formed by ch 1, dtr), [7 dc in next ch-sp] 19 times; join with sl st in top of beginning ch-3—20 7-dc

mixed motif Cami

LARGE SQUARE

groups. Fasten off B.

Rnd 10 Join A in first dc of any 7-dc group, ch 1, sc in same st, [ch 1, sk 1 dc, sc in next dc] 3 times, ch 1, * sc in first dc of next 7-dc group, [ch 1, sk 1 dc, sc in next dc] 3 times, ch 1; repeat from * around; join with sl st in first sc—80 ch-1 sp. Do not fasten off.

First corner

Row 1 (begin corner) Sl st in first ch-1 sp, ch 1, sc in same sp, [ch 1, sk 1 sc, sc in next ch-1 sp] 19 times; leave rem ch-sps unworked—20 sc and 19 ch-sps.

Row 2 Ch 1, turn, sc in first ch-1 sp, [ch 2, sk 1 sc, sc in next ch-1 sp] 11 times; leave rem ch-sps unworked—12 sc and 11 ch-sp.

Row 3 Ch 1, turn, sc in first ch-sp, [ch 2, sk 1 sc, sc in next ch-sp] across—11 sc and 10 ch-sp.

Rows 4–12 Repeat Row 3 having 1 less sc and 1 less ch-sp each row—2 sc and 1 ch-sp at end of Row 12.

Row 13 Turn, sc in ch-sp. Fasten off.

mixed motif Cami

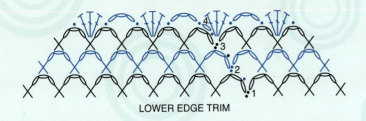
LOWER EDGE TRIM

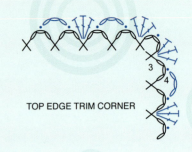
TOP EDGE TRIM CORNER

Next corner
For second, third and fourth corner, join A in first ch-sp to the left of 20th sc of previous corner. Repeat Rows 1-13.

Finishing
Take care to keep the motifs in place while joining. You may wish to pin the motifs to the outline.

Joining
Note The number of chains needed for each chain space should be selected to ensure that the pieces stay in place and lie flat. In most cases, ch 3 or ch 4 is sufficient. In the instruction below for joining, the phrase "work chs" means to work the number of chs needed to span the distance to next motif.
Join yarn with sl st in any st or sp of any motif, * work chs, sl st in adjoining motif; rep from * until all motifs are joined. When all motifs of both front and back pieces are completely joined, join side edges in same manner.

Lower edge trim
Join A with sl st in any st or sp along lower edge.
Rnd 1 Ch 3, [sk 1 sp or st, sc in next sp or st, ch 3] evenly spaced around; ensure that you have an even number of ch-3 sps; join with sl st in base of beginning ch-3.
Rnds 2 and 3 Sl st in first ch-3 sp, ch 3, [sc in next ch-3 sp, ch 3] around; join with sl st in first sl st.
Rnd 4 Sl st in first ch-3 sp, ch 1, sl st in same sp, [ch 3, sl st in next ch-3 sp, 3 dc in next sc, sl st in next ch-3 sp] around; join with sl st in first sl st to join. Fasten off.

Top edge trim
Join A with sl st in sp or st at either underarm and work trim along first
underarm, neck and second underarm.
Rnds 1 and 2 Work as for Rnds 1 and 2 of lower edge trim.
Rnd 3 Work as for Rnd 3 of lower edge trim, working [sc, ch 3, sc] in each top corner of front and back.
Rnd 4 Work as for Rnd 4 of lower edge trim, working [3 dc in next sc, sl st in next ch-3 sp, 3 dc in next sc] in each top corner of front and back.
For straps, slip ends of leather laces through ch-3 sps of Rnd 3 of top edge trim. Sew side seams.

Weave in all ends.

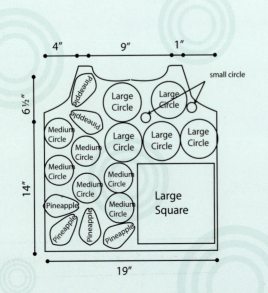

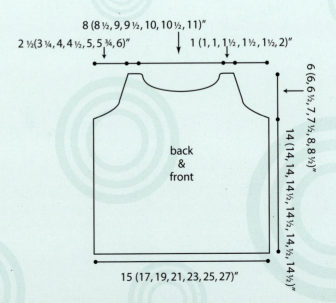